"I've been inspired by Erica Tanov's quietly refined visual sensibility since I discovered her work. *Design by Nature* offers a fascinating look at her creative process and her sources of inspiration, illustrated with beautiful, soulful photography by Ngoc Minh Ngo."

JULIE CARLSON, founder of Remodelista and author of *Remodelista*

"It is a joy to look through Erica Tanov's lens; she's a kindred spirit and steward on the path of amplifying the source of our creativity. Designing and aligning with nature, that higher intelligence, is the essence of balance that begins within each of us."

PAULETTE COLE, cofounder and creative director of ABC Carpet and Home

"There is hardly anything I like more than getting that rare glimpse inside the process, not to mention the very space in which an artist works. *Design by Nature* shows exactly how Erica works and what she is inspired by. Few artists are this open in sharing their inspirations. I find that only the truly confident ones do it well."

TODD HIDO, photographer and artist

"Erica is a mix master. As a designer and artist, she picks references from nature and beautifully weaves them into her home, stores, and gorgeous designs. There is a sublime earthy, yet ephemeral combination that is Erica's special gift to design. This beautiful book captures that rare combination and gives you a perfect glimpse into the amazing creative mind of this true talent."

CHRISTIANE LEMIEUX, founder and creative director of DwellStudio and author of *The Finer Things* and *Undecorate*

# DESIGN BY NATURE

# DESIGN BY NATURE

creating layered, lived-in spaces inspired by the natural world

ERICA TANOV

Photographs by Ngoc Minh Ngo

TEN SPEED PRESS
California | New York

If you truly love nature, you will find beauty everywhere.

—VINCENT VAN GOGH

# CONTENTS

The real voyage of discovery consists not in seeking
new landscapes but in having new eyes.

—MARCEL PROUST

## Introduction: A Way of Seeing

It's what we notice.

Often it's the little details and everyday things that inspire me most.

Like the heart-shaped crack in the sidewalk that I see on walks with my
dog, Lily. As the seasons change, the heart remains but its contents vary.
Encrusted with dirt and pebbles in the summer or with a bit of moss
peeking out after a fresh rain, it never fails to fill me with wonder.

While I find inspiration everywhere—art, movies, travel, people—nature is
my primary muse and the anchor for my creativity. I grew up in California,
a place of extraordinary natural beauty, so nature has always been at the
core of my inspiration and has influenced my aesthetic.
I love being outside. It's where I feel most alive, grounded,
and at peace.

My design process
begins with observing
my surroundings.

My design process begins with observing my surroundings.
Nature can inspire me literally—a plant I see and draw can
reemerge in a print—or abstractly—the dense colors of overlapping foliage
can appear as a color scheme; the curling, folding edges of a leaf as a ruffled
hem. The natural world also inspires the spirit of my work. Being in the
presence of nature grounds me and gives me the calm temperament that
allows me to begin the creative process.

My appreciation for nature and the ability to observe probably began
with the hikes my sister, Eden, and I would take with our dad. Being
surrounded by the majestic trees and fragrances of the forest while we
explored the winding paths filled me with awe. We'd stop for lunch in
a secluded nook of the trail, perching on large rocks or tree stumps,

pretending to be wood nymphs. Eden and I would pop cherry tomatoes into our mouths, pressing our ears against each other's cheeks to hear the little tomato explode as we bit down, amazed that such a huge sound and sensation could come from such a small, succulent thing. These early childhood times spent outside in places that I loved solidified my relationship with the natural world.

I was also finding inspiration in my everyday surroundings. As a young girl, I would tag along with my aunt to the flea markets where I discovered the love of the hunt. I remember once finding a sack of old embroidered linens. Although they were stained and riddled with holes, I beamed with pride over my purchase because I'd paid only a few dollars for the whole bag. Looking at the doilies, my dad commented that I should seek out quality over quantity (a philosophy I took to heart). Still, there was something I loved about the old fabrics; the history they held and the stories they told, stains and all. I didn't know what I would do with them, but I had a budding hope of making something beautiful.

I showed an early love of decorating interior spaces. When I was in second grade, my mom, who had always provided me with an abundance of art supplies, encouraged me to plan and choose the decor for my new room. I had a vision of creating a magical secret garden. I picked out an orange-and-pink-flowered wallpaper, thrilled to have stripes and vines of happy flowers climbing toward the ceiling. I chose a grass-green shag carpet so it would look as if the flowers were growing from the floor.

A few years later, my grandfather built a dollhouse just for me. With my initials—E.T.—carved into the front door and a secret drop-down stairway from the attic—features he designed—it felt very special. I remember spending so much time deciding on the wallpaper and getting lost in creating a whole world, miniature but still complete. I created accessories to complement the furniture my grandpa had made; little cookie sheets from chipboard and tin foil and baked tiny rolls and cookies that I shellacked so they would keep. I used vintage handkerchiefs I found at the flea market as monogrammed sheets on the beds. Designing a space where I had artistic control was a formative experience for me. Being granted the freedom to create my own environment helped me establish a solid sense of my artistic self from a very young age.

When I was twelve, I began taking sewing classes. I was very small for my age and was still wearing kid-size clothing when everyone else was moving into the teen section. So I started making my own clothes. I became known as an eclectic dresser, putting together unusual outfits, mixing prints and patterns and vintage pieces I was starting to collect. In high school, I can vividly recall making myself a ruffled floral miniskirt out of upholstery fabric, which I wore with an army-green cotton-twill bomber jacket (that I also made), a white cotton blouse with a ruffled collar, and my gold Esprit ballet flats. I loved this outfit because of its unlikely mix of silhouettes, textures, and colors.

My fashion sense became more refined over time and, after I graduated from Parsons School of Design in New York, I went to work for fashion designer Rebecca Moses. After two years of working on Seventh Avenue, I became disillusioned with certain aspects of the fashion world and wanted to do something that allowed a more personal expression of my creativity but wasn't quite sure what that would be.

I took on various jobs—assisting stylists, working for a milliner—and spent time hanging out in cafés with my journal, pondering my next move. During that time, I started designing and sewing lingerie inspired by vintage pieces I had collected from regular flea-market hunts and a pair of my grandfather's monogrammed silk pajamas that I had inherited. I was combining elements that were important to me: fine craftsmanship, subtle old-world details, and timeless styles.

Once I had a small collection of samples, I decided to take them around to my favorite stores, starting in Soho and then scheduling appointments with Henri Bendel and Barneys. It was different back in 1990. Buyers were much more eager to meet with young, unknown designers, enchanted by viewing their wares out of a vintage suitcase. These meetings led to orders—more than I expected—and soon I was in full production: making patterns, sewing, shipping, invoicing. I had a business. I was a designer.

As my business grew, so did my yearning for a more relaxed lifestyle. After nine years in New York, I was ready to return to California and open my first store. Dragging my soon-to-be-husband, Steven, a musician and composer, along, we moved to Berkeley into a building that once housed my grandfather's laundry business—a building full of memories and history that felt like the ideal place to continue growing my business and start our new life together on the West Coast.

Being back in California, surrounded by natural beauty, sparked new ideas and creativity. I began designing my own prints, which was a new medium for expression, and gradually ventured from lingerie and clothing into home goods—pillows, bedding, tablecloths, and, eventually, wallpaper and furniture.

A couple of years after moving to Berkeley, Steven and I decided to start a family, and we moved to a sweet Craftsman bungalow to have more space and separation between work and home. We now have two children, Hugo and Isabelle, who are the center of our world. Definitely our greatest collaboration. Being a mother is the most important part of my life, and it has forced me to be less uptight and more relaxed about my style, knowing there will always be some degree of mess. But it doesn't mean I've sacrificed my love of nice things. I have an off-white sofa that the kids jump, eat, and sleep on, and a dining room table covered in water rings and bits of paint and markers. We really *live* in our house, and I love that about it. I've never felt as if I had to sacrifice style in order to have a home where people feel comfortable. Our house is beautiful but not pristine. I never allow things to be too precious, and I anticipate that something will eventually become stained or broken.

> I steer away from anything too perfect or manicured and prefer to create beautiful, relaxed spaces by embracing objects with their imperfections.

As a collector with a minimalist husband, I've learned to balance my penchant for amassing beautiful objects with his desire for simplicity by being selective in filling our home only with things I truly love and feel a deep connection to. Over time, I've curated my stores in the same way—by choosing well-crafted pieces, and combining them to create a sense of lived-in grandeur.

A writer once described me as an "imperfectionist," and it rings true. I steer away from anything too perfect or manicured and prefer to create beautiful, relaxed spaces by embracing objects with their imperfections. I'm basically

a refined hippie—attracted to the loose, natural, and raw and things in disrepair—yet am also drawn to pieces with a hint of glamour and opulence. I believe in buying high-quality goods although the name of the maker or designer is not important. I buy lasting things that I love.

Everything I do, from designing clothing or wallpaper to arranging a room, aspires to reflect the effortless beauty of the natural world. My designs are often inspired by simple sights: the trees in my backyard, the fallen leaves and blooming flowers I see on my walks, or a single fern casting its shadow on my porch. I love the flawed beauty inherent in nature. Perfectly imperfect. I want everything I design and make to have that same relaxed sensibility.

This is not a "how to" book. . . . Trust your instincts and surround yourself with objects you love that have meaning to you.

My wish is for you to find inspiration in your own surroundings. It isn't about traveling far and wide to beautiful landscapes (although that never hurts), but, rather, it's about discovering beauty right outside your door. It can be something as grand as an old tree with wide-reaching limbs or something as small as a tiny leaf or acorn. You can find inspiration in a weed blowing gracefully on the freeway or the pattern of the craggy bark of an oak tree. You can be moved by the intense ochre colors of lichen growing on a branch or fallen twig or the damp fertile smell after a rain. Everything is source material.

I've arranged the chapters in this book around the elements of nature that are the most important in my work: wood, water, dirt, weeds, and decay. All of these expressions of the enviornment work together in my designs, and overlap with one another. It's not just the obviously celebrated aspects of the outdoors that call to me—perfect flowers and pretty flora—but the overlooked parts too, moss, decomposing leaves, and withering petals. It is nature in its totality that brings so much texture and richness to my world and my work.

This is not a "how to" book. I don't have any design rules to pass on to you. In fact, I don't even believe in design do's and don'ts. You can't teach someone a sense of style. It is for each individual to interpret the world in his or her own way. Trust your instincts and surround yourself with objects you love that have meaning to you.

No matter where you are, beauty of some kind surrounds you. . . . Beauty is everywhere and accessible to everyone.

My design process and the way I style interiors is hugely intuitive—second nature—and my hope is to inspire you to find beauty in the simplest, often overlooked parts of your surroundings, and to bring that beauty into your life, in your own way.

No matter where you are, beauty of some kind surrounds you. You don't have to live in the countryside to discover beauty right outside your door. To me, nature is any environment you find yourself in. Beauty is everywhere and accessible to everyone. I truly believe that.

Whether it's the crack in a sidewalk with a bit of life emerging, a crumbling stone wall, a reflective puddle after the rain, or a grove of redwoods, everyone has access to the beauty of the natural world.

It's the ability to *see* that beauty that's important, and what you do with that beauty that makes you a creative person. And it is also how you bring what inspires you into your life and the life of those around you.

FINDING INSPIRATION

This book is about simply opening all of your senses to what is already in front of you. I hope that these pages help you discover nature's everyday miracles in the seemingly ordinary and that they inspire you to both find and create your own beauty.

# WOOD

Sitting at the desk of my home studio, I gaze out the windows, lost in the countless patterns formed by leaves and light. Once an enclosed sunporch, my creative haven—"the treehouse"—is nestled between the branches of an old oak tree. It's the perfect workspace for me because it brings me into the woods. Looking out at the branches, I'm transported to my childhood, to the weekends when my father would take my sister and me hiking in Berkeley's Tilden Park.

I remember how the redwoods loomed high above us, their tops touching the sky. We walked along the winding trails; the ground, blanketed with pine needles, soft and inviting beneath our feet. Live oaks greeted the sun with their wide reach of branches; the gnarled trunks of native cypress trees twisted in the distance. Rays of sunlight peeked through the canopy, illuminating the warm red bark of the massive redwoods. The air came alive with the perfumes of the forest: ponderosa pines releasing a vanilla aroma, Douglas firs zesting the air with their citrusy resin.

The textures of trees intrigued me: the tapestry of emerald moss growing along trunks; a constellation of woodpecker-pecked holes; the fledgling ferns laced with dew, sprouting from the sides of redwood trunks. I would reach out to touch the rough-looking bark with my small hands, surprised to find it shaggy and soft. I traced its lichen-laced surface with my little fingers.

My sister and I snacked on sunflower seeds, spitting out a trail of shells along the enchanted forest floor, pretending it would help us find our way back home. We traipsed among mossy damp ferns, which unfurled around my tangled unbrushed hair. It was my first place of wonder; there my imagination was set free.

Standing underneath those coast redwoods—the tallest trees in the world— we craned our necks to look up at their height. We stood in reverence, gazing at the feathery boughs of green needles waving in the wind. These ancient trees, present when dinosaurs roamed, inspired in me such a sense of stillness and awe. In their majestic, unwavering presence, I came to a newfound sense of time. They were here long before us and will remain long after we are gone. They deliver me from the smallness of my human existence and expand my ideas about my place in the world and my sense of creation.

I still walk those same woods, among the very same trees. As I wander through the mesmerizing maze of greens and browns, ideas for new textiles emerge in my mind. The pale sage green of hanging lichen and gray of sun-bleached twigs to the deepest dark browns of hollowed out trunks inspire soothing color palettes. Graceful, veering branches crisscrossing against the sky reveal patterns of plaid, stripes, and argyle.

The many textures of bark, from rough oaks and scored birch to peeling eucalyptus, inspire the fabrics I create and work with; rugged weaves such as burlap or raw silk and cotton ikat. Moroccan Beni Ourain rugs remind me of the diamond-patterned surface of an oak tree. Turkish Tulu rugs, made from the long hair of Angora goats, call to mind the shaggy bark of redwood.

Trees anchor me. They are the foundation of my sense of design—the core of my aesthetic. They have taught me that great creativity can emerge from a place of calm and understanding.

I not only look to the physical attributes of trees for inspiration but I also find deep comfort in their presence. I walk among them to find stillness. I bring that serenity and sense of wonder back with me to the drawing table, so that I can create from a place of groundedness.

Trees anchor me. They are the foundation of my sense of design—the core of my aesthetic. They have taught me that great creativity can emerge from a place of calm and understanding. From their puzzle-piece bark rearranging into infinite patterns to their rich textured layers and verdant warm colors, you will find them everywhere in my work.

The fabric shown here pays homage to the patterns I see in tree bark and in the grain of wood. Experimenting with ink and watercolor paintings depicting the trees I see out my window and the collected pieces of bark I find on my walks can lead to graphic and abstract iterations for clothing and textile prints. Metallic gold adds glamour to "tendril" print wallpaper and captures the shimmering surface that remains when bark has been stripped from the trunks of trees.

Something as simple as a bisected log can provide endless inspiration. The rings, which chronicle events in the natural world (wider rings speak of abundant rainfall; thin ones mark times of drought), have become a design theme of circular motifs for pillows on my sofa. The graying beiges and browns of the drying wood inspire the warm, tonal color palette of the room.

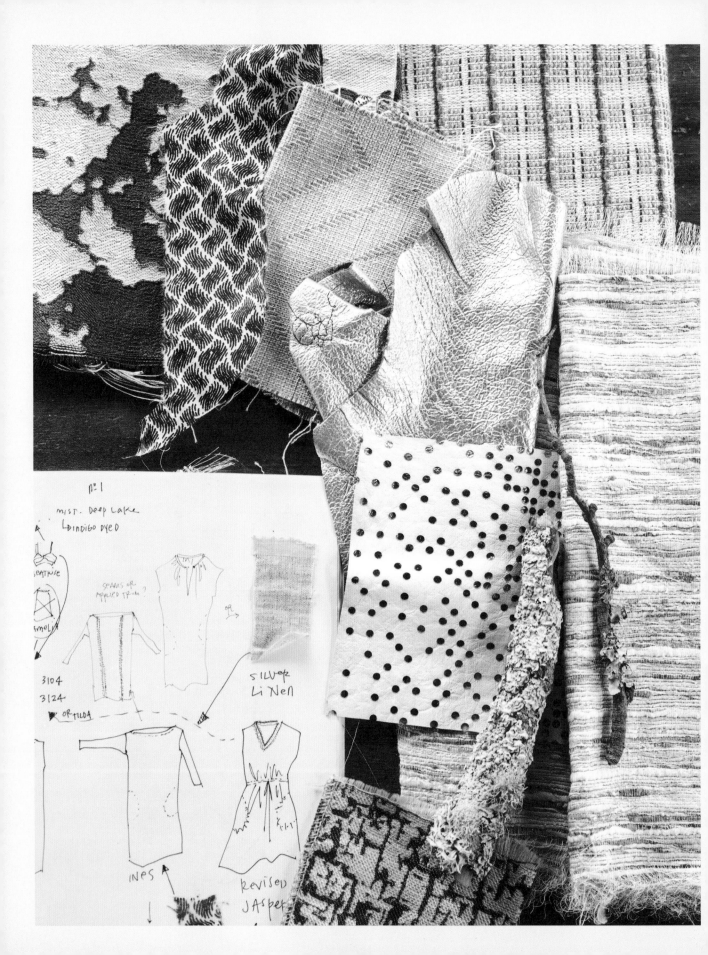

I love playing with the textural nature of wood. In one particular collection, I layered textures and patterns: raw silk reminiscent of birch trees, perforated leather representing wood-pecked holes, a dotted jamdani cotton capturing the dappled light that peeks through the fluttering leaves, jacquard fabrics depicting the bark of a craggy oak and the mottled pattern of a sycamore.

Both the seagrass wall covering and the Indian raw silk of the "Hedra" coat, one of my favorite styles inspired by a coat of my mother's from the 1960s, remind me of scored birch trees.

## DESIGN NOTES
## Trees as Memory Keepers

My neighbors recently removed some trees from their property. I sat completely mesmerized at my window, watching the arborist climb to the very top, methodically strapping and then sawing each limb, working his way down. I longed to be up in that tree. Not to cut it down but to experience its magnificence so completely. I felt sad watching this tree, which I'm sure had been witness to so much, come down in pieces.

Soon after, while on a walk in Tilden Park, I passed a bench near Jewel Lake. Over the years, people have carved their initials into the wood, marking their presence. I think of all the little crushes and moments that will last, possibly only because they are held by the wood. These twin images—the tree coming down and the bench preserving memories—remind me of the cycle of nature, how one thing gone can reemerge. When I walk by that bench, I remember that life carries on and that stories and memories are tucked into the world around us.

About two years ago, I took a fascinating weaving class. Having received a small loom as part of the class fee, I was able to begin making my own weavings at home using fibers I had on hand from my past collections. I took scraps of fabric and pulled them apart, unraveling each strand of yarn. I used the yarn to experiment with in my weavings, as well as remaining pieces of leather and seam binding. Any piece of fabric or trim I could find, even extra sequins, were woven into these tapestries. This was not only a way for me to be resourceful but also a way to remember my previous work and stay in touch with it, giving it new life in this new context and form.

Tufted aged leather of the chairs from Swiss designer
Kurt Thut remind me of the cracking knots in wood. The
irregular diamond pattern of the Moroccan Beni Ourain
shag rug closely resembles the bark of an oak tree.

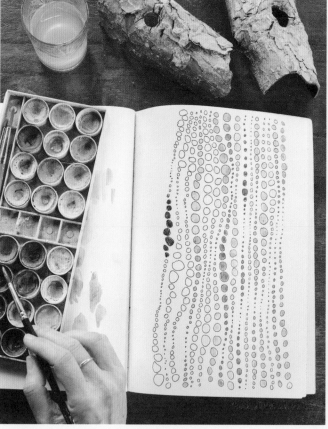

Collecting lichen-covered twigs and moss-laden
branches inspires a sophisticated color palette
of ochre, greys.

ARTIST SPOTLIGHT
## *Janelle Pietrzak*

The time came for new dressing-room curtains in my Fourth Street store in Berkeley. I imagined textural panels that were both raw and refined, resembling the magnificence of trees; a blend of hippie and glamour in which hand-woven elements would be incorporated. I envisioned weaving them myself, but soon realized I had neither the expertise nor a large-enough loom to do so. Instead, I contacted my weaving guru, Janelle Pietrzak, to see if she would want to collaborate on this project. After describing my vision of a super-textural and tonal weaving with touches of metallic gold and her trademark tassels, she sent me a bevy of cream- and beige-toned yarns of varying thickness and sheen to choose from. Once I selected the yarns, Janelle created stunning woven panels made of looped and tasseled cotton rope, fibrous hemp, fluffy roving, and a touch of shimmery smooth viscose. She also wove in gold yarn that I had given her—left over from sweaters I had designed—and applied gold foil to the finished weaving for added opulence.

The two continuous curtain panels hang side by side, creating a textural tree-like landscape with a beautiful knotted tassel base that captures the essence of tree roots. With hints of shimmering gold thread woven throughout, the curtains are glamorous yet understated and impart the raw and regal beauty of trees, capturing both their rich texture and stately presence.

thick
flat weave
cotton fiber
Gold leaf

Puffs &
floats-organic
natural texture

organic
weave texture
with bits of
gold yarn

thicker flat
weave-cotton
fiber

mixed fiber
loopy Rope ar

57"

26"

Viscose
& thick

thicker flat

organic
texture

The languorous quality of lichen hanging from trees
reminds me of tassels on the edge of a curtain or fringe
of a wall hanging. Its tangled hair-like nature inspires
the shaggy pillows made from brushed alpaca yarn.

All it has experienced, tasted, suffered:

the course of years, generations of animals,

oppression, recovery, friendship of sun and wind

will pour forth each day in the song of its rustling foliage,

in the friendly gesture of its gently swaying crown, in

the delicate sweet scent of resinous sap moistening the sleep-

glued buds, and the eternal game of lights and

shadows it plays with itself, content.

—HERMANN HESSE

# WATER

I have spent most of my life in the San Francisco Bay Area, surrounded by water and blanketed by fog. In the mornings, I watch the fog through my bedroom window, wrapping its diaphanous fingers around the trees. It slinks through the landscape like flowing gossamer, draping itself across buildings, billowing across the ocean's surface. It moves gently and elusively throughout the city until the sun burns it away, and then it is gone.

*At certain hours of the day, there is the magic spectacle of sunlight hitting the waves; which sparkle as if someone has scattered thousands of sequins across their surface.*

Living in California makes me aware of how precious water is. When there is drought, rain feels like a benediction. All the plants perk up with gratitude, and a sense of hope returns to the ground. The rain falls down, and my backyard is awash with life.

Water, of course, *is* life. It is the element that allows everything to flourish. Everything I've come to love about nature—trees, flowers, weeds, soil—all depend on water.

Since I was little, we've been going up to my family's cabin in Soda Springs each summer. A short walk from our cabin is an area of the Yuba River that we've named "The Flat Rock" because of its massive smooth-stone shore. While my mom read and sunbathed, my sister and I would challenge each other to cross the rushing waters, hopscotching from boulder to boulder. We would pause, bringing our cupped hands down to the river's edge, taking a sip of the cool, pure water.

There is a swimming hole in the river, with a rope swing hanging from a large tilting pine. I'd climb up the rope, my bare feet clutching its end, and swing out over the deep green water, letting go and plunging into the icy depths. I can still feel that sensation of initial shock as the cold water enveloped my body. For a brief moment, the darkness would hold me, until I came darting up to the surface, arms aloft, invigorated, cleansed, wildly alive.

My sister and I were also obsessed with skipping stones, and we would search for the smoothest, flattest ones, taking turns skimming them across the river's surface. I was mesmerized by the rings each stone created against the still face of the water. The pattern of growing circles was something I never tired of, watching the continuous formation of rings moving outward and outward toward the edge.

I have always been captivated by the way water moves—how the liquid lines of a stream change course, looping back on themselves; the infinite swirls and tiny whirlpools pirouetting like ballet dancers. There is a feminine quality to the way water travels downstream, curvy lines undulating toward the sea, braiding themselves together as they journey to the ocean.

To be ever-changing is the essential nature of water; to be everywhere and in all forms, at once—a roiling ocean, a cloud, and a still pool. When I'm stuck creatively, water's clear nature is an invitation to see with new eyes, a fluid reminder to shift shapes and forms. To be untethered, free, and flowing.

The gentle rocking of the ocean draws me in; the lulling metronome of its tides ebbing and flowing. I love the frothy whitecaps and the ombre effect of the pale sky bleeding into the blue water. At certain hours of the day, there is the magic spectacle of sunlight hitting the waves; which sparkle as if someone has scattered thousands of sequins across their surface. When the evening tide is going out, there's a calmness as the sea washes up onto the shore and pulls other treasures out with it.

I'm also drawn to the stillness of water, the way it comes to rest in lakes and ponds, like a mirror reflecting the natural world around it. In the surface of a still lake, you can watch clouds drift by, experience the sun set, and see the reflections of trees dancing in the wind.

Water's many colors and forms instruct my designs, from white-whipped waves and pale oceans to the shimmering quality of sunlight on the surface.

Its shapes and movements appear in my work: waves inspire the scalloped edge of a dress or a motif for a print, eerie morning fog influences diaphanous gauze curtains, an indigo-dyed pillow echoes the horizon meeting the sea. Much of the clothing I design has a loose, flowing quality inspired directly by the nature of water. I want a silk gown to move with the same ease as a flowing stream.

To be ever-changing is the essential nature of water; to be everywhere and in all forms, at once—a roiling ocean, a cloud, and a still pool. When I'm stuck creatively, water's clear nature is an invitation to see with new eyes, a fluid reminder to shift shapes and forms. To be untethered, free, and flowing.

DESIGN NOTES
## Water Prints

For my autumn 2017 collection, I used work by Oakland-based artist Kelly Ording to create prints for clothing and bedding.

Like me, Kelly grew up in the Bay Area and is heavily influenced by the water that surrounds us. As a child, she spent a lot of time at the beach or near the bay; as a result, water is a constant theme in her work. Her paintings and line drawings are a perfect blend of precise control and organic ease; and I love her ability to play with perfection and the unknown—bold yet delicate graphic lines that are layered onto coffee-dyed paper and canvases. Her work is meditative in its use of repetitive linear motifs and negative space. It's these characteristics that remind me of the serenity of a deep lake at sunset and the ebb and flow of the calm ocean.

Denim is a perfect year-round, timeless fabric both in fashion
and interiors that can be mixed with almost anything. I like to
leave the edges raw or expose selvages for added texture and
a more relaxed and casual feel.

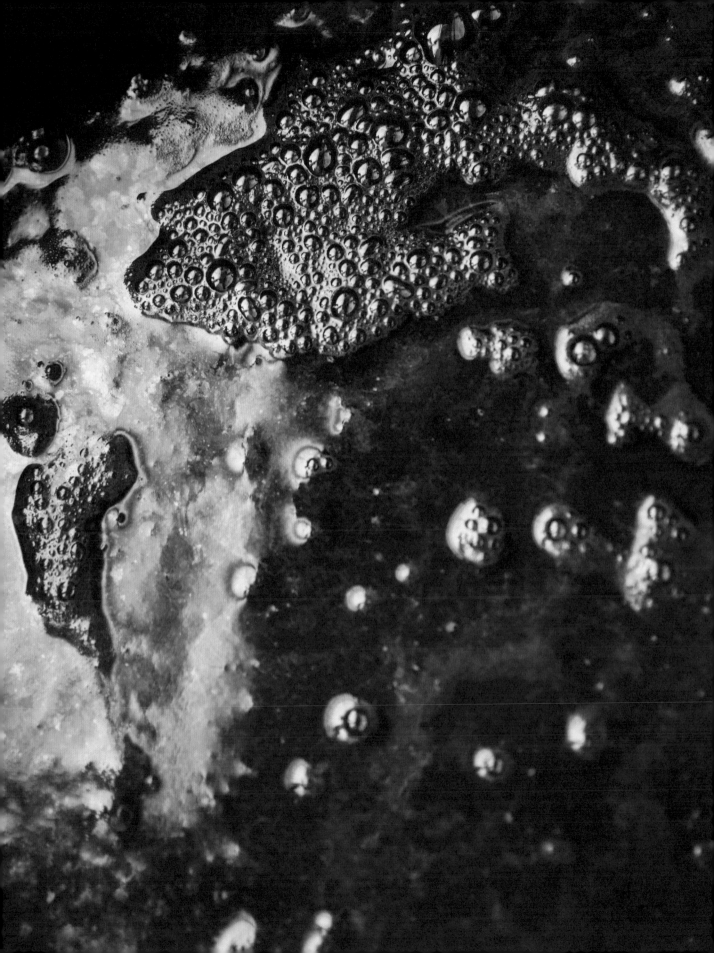

ARTIST SPOTLIGHT
*Sierra Reading*

I've long been intrigued by natural dyes and have dabbled in learning about them by taking indigo dyeing classes and natural plants dye tours at the University of California Botanical Garden. There is so much to know and learn about natural dyes that when I wanted to incorporate indigo dyeing into one of my collections to evoke the color, movement, and depth of the ocean, I knew I needed to approach someone who had a wealth of experience and knowledge. I reached out to textile artist and fifth-generation Northern Californian Sierra Reading.

Sierra works exclusively with plant-derived dyes to create seasonal color collections for a variety of designers. While so many of today's indigo dyes are made synthetically, true natural indigo is made through a process of drying and composting indigo leaves into a blue pigment that is then fermented. Natural dyes typically come from bark, leaves, or berries that are reduced down through boiling, but making indigo dye is more challenging. It's a complex process, and keeping a steady supply of indigo alive requires attention and expertise. Because the dye is a living organism, the dyer must care for it—feeding it and keeping it warm and active. Sierra always has a vat of indigo brewing in her studio.

When dyeing fabric with indigo, the dyer submerges the cloth into the dye, which turns the material a yellowish green, but as the fabric re-enters the air, it turns blue. For an even darker blue, the dyer repeats the dipping process, building layers of blue.

I wanted to have a variety of patterns within the collection, ranging from ombré (achieved by dip-dyeing) to stripes and diamonds. Sierra employed a few different techniques—using wood blocks, tying and twisting, and dipping—to achieve a group of distinct designs. The result was a collection that perfectly captured the colors, spirit, and movement of water.

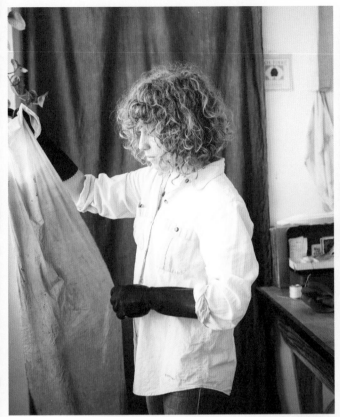

## ARTIST SPOTLIGHT
### *Emily Payne*

Emily Payne has a true gift—the ability to express the many forms that a single object can embody, stretching ideas and themes in ways I could never imagine. She explores dimensionality, movement, and pattern through wire sculptures, gouache paintings, line drawings, and collage. When I first saw Emily's work, I was completely captivated by the subtlety and the soft, layered quality.

We first decided to collaborate in 2012. We selected pieces of Emily's artwork that we felt would translate beautifully and unexpectedly into fabric and then created four unique prints for my autumn 2012 clothing and bedding collections. My favorite print from this collaboration was the "wave print," which was based on one of Emily's collage pieces made from layers of linen torn from the vintage book covers that she collects. We reduced the size of the original work and developed a pattern that repeated along the expanse of the fabric, creating a calming oceanic effect. I had it printed on cotton for quilts, pillowcases, tablecloths, and napkins and on silk for kaftans, blouses, and slips. Delicate flickers of gold foil were added to the silk, portraying the shimmering surface of the ocean.

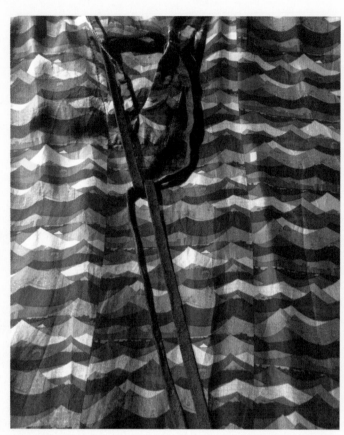 

The room is prepared, the incense burned.

I close the shutters before I close my eyelids.

The patterns of the quilt repeat the waters of the river.

The gauze curtain is like a mist.

Then a dream comes to me and when I awake

I no longer know where I am.

I open the western window and watch the waves

Stretching on and on to the horizon.

—SU TUNG P'O

DESIGN NOTES
## Shimmering Wall

In 2010, I opened a store in Marin County, CA. The new space was completely raw and required total build-out, so I brought in architect and friend Douglas Burnham of Envelope A+D. I wanted the store to feel relaxed and luxurious without being overly designed. We hand selected the walnut, bay laurel, and cypress slabs that would become tables and embedded shelving and benches. We used the leftover pieces for the exterior hanging signs. Envelope A+D designed a stunning case made of oxidized metal, walnut, and glass to showcase jewelry. The creamy hand-plastered walls created a warm and inviting environment. To finish the space, I wanted a dramatic focal point when entering the store—something spectacular mounted on one of the walls.

During the planning and construction, I made several trips back and forth from my studio in Berkeley to the Marin store location, crossing the Richmond–San Rafael bridge. I noticed that when heading back to Berkeley, if I ascended the bridge around 11 a.m., the late-morning light would hit the water just right, creating a moment of magic—the sunlight sparkling on the surface. It struck me that the wall in the store should represent that shimmering effect of the light on the bay.

Not long after this epiphany, while standing in my closet, I saw one of my favorite evening bags hanging from a hook. A drawstring-cinched fabric pouch covered in brass paillettes. Seeing the brass discs catch the light, I knew I had come upon the dawning of the store backdrop: an entire wall of layered brass sequins. The golden surface of the metal discs and their subtle movement would provide the sparkle I was imagining. I brought the purse to my next meeting at Envelope A+D and explained my vision to the team, and they set to work. Thousands of 3-inch oval brass discs were custom made and then each one was hand hammered into the wall with small brass nails, taking a week to install. The effect was magical.

They hang against the south wall facing the entrance of the store, enveloping it in a gentle, shimmering glow. I still make my weekly drives over the bridge and try to time my return just right so I get to experience that brilliant sparkling of the bay, when the sun is hitting the water at that perfect angle, and the surface becomes a blanket of shimmering sequins.

# DIRT

I've always been a tactile person. As a child, I used to carry around a small quilt, constantly rubbing the soft cotton between my fingertips until it became nothing but shreds of fabric and batting. So, it's no surprise that I prefer to garden without gloves; reveling in the texture of the earth on my hands, the rich soil crumbling through my fingers, sorting through roots and stones. I like how it gets underneath my fingernails, leaving chestnut-colored crescent moons at the ends of my fingertips.

Dirt is one of those elements of nature that is often overlooked. Less showy than flora and not as majestic as trees, it is still a deep source of inspiration for my work. I'm captivated by the way the ground is constantly changing—cracking in a drought, fertile after the rain. I'm lured by the rich, seductive colors of the terrain: dark basalt, burnt umber, henna, the auburn glow of terra-cotta.

*Using elements that come from the earth, roots these fabrics directly to the native landscape.*

So many textiles elicit the nature of dirt. The dampness of soil reminds me of suede. Rich mud calls to mind sultry velvet. Dry, rocky dirt is like coarsely woven linen embellished with beads or shells. Many primitive tapestries and indigenous woven fabrics are made from plant dyes and the fibers of the earth itself, like shaggy chamula, a traditional Mexican textile often dyed with mud. Since the times of the Roman Empire, oak galls have been used for making ink and natural dye, creating a beautiful purply brown color. Using elements that come from the earth, roots these fabrics directly to the native landscape.

Dirt is also like the earth's canvas, dotted with the footprints of the creatures who travel its surface. The primal patterns found on antique rugs and tribal textiles often look like animal tracks embossed into the ground cover. While the primitive symbols and how they are arranged in African mud cloth (or bogolanfini) tell a secret story, to me, the simple hatch marks look like a bird's footprint, and the maze-like motifs resemble the tunneling patterns that beetles leave behind. The lines of cracked dried earth are conveyed in a Peruvian Diamanta throw and the zigzag, labyrinth-like patterns of Kuba cloth remind me of fallen twigs on the forest floor. I find that decorating with these traditional tapestries connects the interiors of homes to the natural world.

The ground is also where I find my treasures. Beauty can often be found just by looking down. The earth's surface is like a natural flea market, and I am a collector. On walks with my dog, Lily, I am constantly stopping to pick things up off the ground, endlessly discovering gifts that lay in plain sight. Bits of nature's offerings that are ready for the taking.

Beauty can often be found just by looking down. The earth's surface is like a natural flea market, and I am a collector.

I come across magnolia cones attached to their velvety brown stems, sometimes the curly stigmas still intact, appearing as miniature works of art—tiny, intricate sculptures. I can't resist collecting these. I also gather samara wings (or helicopters) that have fluttered to the ground from a bigleaf maple, the spiky fruits of the sweetgum tree, and the nubby, solid-looking sycamore spheres that can fall apart into thousands of cotton-haired seeds at the slightest touch. The fragrant blue-white domed fruit of eucalyptus also call to me, needing to be picked up. Inspiration is readily available if we simply pay attention.

I come home and empty my pockets, laying my botanical findings on any available surface. Already lining the windowsills of my home are delicate lichen-covered twigs, the deep umber calyxes of flowers, fallen capped acorns, a bird's lost feather. I often sketch these little pieces of nature, turning those

Inspiration is readily available if we simply pay attention.

drawings into prints and patterns for fabric that will one day become clothing or bedding, or even inspiration for a wallpaper pattern. Sometimes it's simply a tiny detail that sparks an idea. The split-open interior of a seedpod can inspire a geometric print, or scattered pebbles can transform into the texture of a beaded pillow. Mostly, it's this feeling I get from dirt—the earthiness, grit, raw beauty—that inspires me to create layered spaces with deep, sultry colors and primitive, graphic patterns. It's the fertility of the earth, that eternal creative place, that I want to translate into my work: the warmth, richness, and mystery.

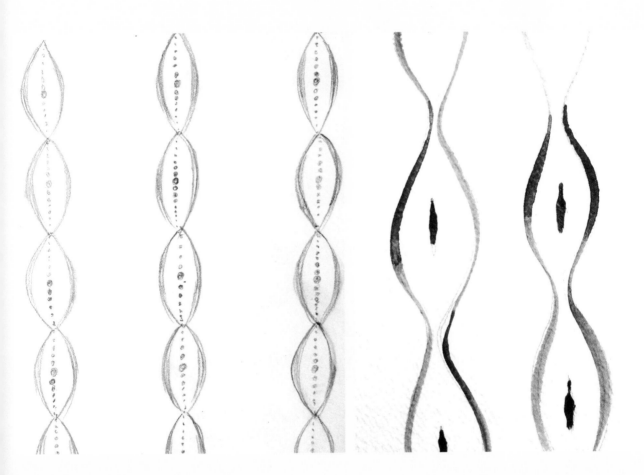

A pencil drawing of seedpods leads to simplified, graphic iterations that may make their way to prints for fabric or wallpaper. You don't have to be an artist to notice details; even quick, simple sketches make you look more closely and appreciate nature's nuances.

Creating an earthy tabletop setting: The looped woven texture and metallic Mukaish embroidery pattern of this Indian textile-turned-table runner remind me of the earth's surface. An assortment of ceramic vessels, some used as vases, others to hold fruit, are casually placed, echoing nature's fallen treasures.

Inspired by a forest floor strewn with leaves and pine cones, I casually tossed pillows in earth tones and graphic patterns onto a daybed to create a relaxed and inviting room.

I am a collector of many things, whether it's nature's offerings that I pick up off the ground, things I find washed ashore, or bibelots scored at a flea market. Here, I lay out a collection of vintage ethnic treasures from a recent estate sale. I come home and arrange my haul to appreciate each object in a new context. I then decide which pieces I can't live without and which I will let go of.

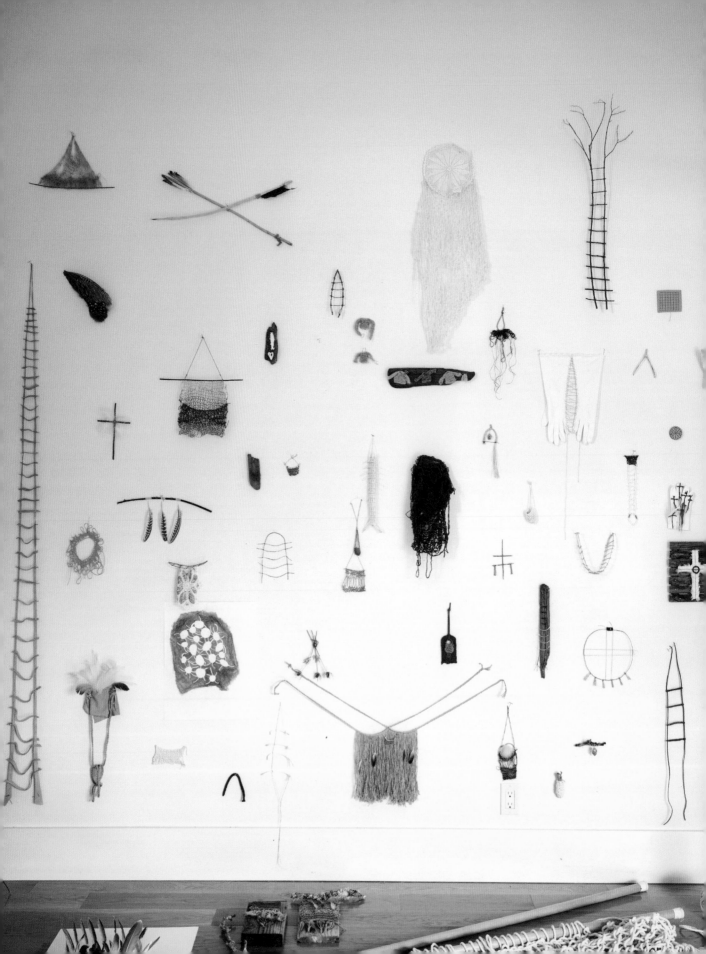

## *Caroline Seckinger*

Artist Caroline Seckinger has worked in many mediums, from drawing, printmaking, and sculpture to film and dance. I am especially moved by her recent work that integrates the elements she collects from the earth around her. Bones, feathers, animal skins, and stones are woven into her wall sculptures, each piece telling a story. Here, Caroline talks a bit about her process.

"This work emerges through a conversation with the land surrounding the studio. It is a language vibrating between the stars and the water. Occasionally there are gifts . . . sky offerings found in the palm of dirt . . . feathers, lichen-laced walnut branches, cypress skin, apple twigs, galls, cones, twisting pods, eggshells, beetles or the decomposing deer bone, stone, a tractor bolt—all on their slow march into soil. I track the threads of how these gifts of the winged, the four-legged, the one-legged sentient kin are within the web of life, and then the poetry of each is woven. It is held, tied, knitted, or knotted with cotton, flax, wool, silk, or leather. For many years, I have been drawn to work in traditional feminine forms of labor. The repetitive nature of handwork is like a mantra. These ancient gestures activate the DNA holding the memories of many grandmothers. I am not nearly as disciplined as they were; I drop, twist, and skip stitches, and the mechanics become organic. Because the works are more like gestures than sculpture, some are made in a few hours or days, akin to the pages of a journal; I call this The Journal Wall."

The color palette of fallen autumn leaves inspires a still life on a mid-century credenza. The organic, rough-hewn ceramic vessels by Akio Nukaga sit upon a vintage hand-loomed Navajo textile, which contrasts with the glossy photo by Rafael Neff.

DESIGN NOTES
## Tribal Textiles

I've been collecting vintage textiles for years. Some I find when traveling but most I buy at estate sales and flea markets. I'm especially drawn to hand-woven tribal textiles. I usually just buy things I like, not necessarily knowing the origin or history of the piece. I've been learning as I go, picking up bits of information where I can. While the beauty and craftsmanship is reason enough for me to buy and cherish something, understanding the process and knowing the origin and original purpose of the piece makes it even more meaningful. It's astounding and humbling to find out what goes into the making of each textile.

Boldly graphic and textural, Kuba cloth is an embroidered and appliquéd fabric of the Kuba people in the Congo. The base cloth is an undecorated square of plain raffia fabric. The men gather and pound raffia leaves to make them soft and malleable. They then weave the cloth on single-heddle looms, which can take days. Typically, the women handle the laborious decoration of the cloth, which involves dyeing, creating detailed needlework, and clipping individual tufts to form the cut-pile embroidery. They follow their inspiration, designing as they go rather than mapping out a pattern beforehand, and so making each piece unique. One small square of Kuba embroidery takes about a month to complete; the designs are usually geometric or maze-like yet deliberately asymmetrical. Kuba cloth was originally made for ceremonial occasions and court rituals and today is often used for funeral celebrations. It has become popular in home décor as wall hangings and also makes strikingly graphic pillows. I love the neutral color palette and heavily textured nature of this art form.

Bolivian mantas (or aguayo) are small hand-woven wool blankets traditionally used by the Andean people to carry infants or dry goods—like the original grocery tote. They're typically made in black or dark brown wool with colorful detailing using all-natural dyes, often with animal motifs, each identifying the region of origin. For thousands of years, these woven textiles have been a mainstay of Andean culture, and while they're used in a utilitarian fashion,

they are also beautiful works of art, sometimes used as altar cloths or wall hangings. Each blanket is incredibly time consuming to make, beginning with raising the sheep, shearing and spinning the wool, dyeing the yarn with plants, and then weaving on handmade looms. They are made to last a lifetime, or several lifetimes, and to serve a variety of purposes. I am drawn to their deep, practical beauty. I use them as table runners or small throws on a sofa or chair. I've yet to carry a baby with one.

The Baluchi people, who live primarily in the Iranian plateau in Pakistan, Iran, and Afghanistan, weave saddlebags to cover their animals and hold supplies as they move through the surrounding mountainous areas. These bags, made from sheeps' wool, densely woven with a thick pile and often adorned with colorful tassels, exhibit traditional design and patterns, which reflect a long history and culture. I cherish these products because they are unique pieces from a disappearing tradition. People often cut them in half to make pillows, but I like keeping them intact, using them as small rugs or throwing them over the edge of the sofa to add some depth and earthiness to a room.

The Banjara, a seminomadic ethnic group throughout the Indian subcontinent (and considered the original gypsies of India), produce colorful textiles that feature delicate appliqué work, intricate embroidery, and inset mirrors, all of which results in elaborate patterns. I love the texture of the coarse cotton weave combined with the dense threadwork and smooth mirrors, which are believed to reflect the evil eye and protect the owner from harm. The material is often embellished with cowrie shell "fringe"—usually seen as a border surrounding the fabric—which acts as a frame for these small works of art that celebrate the strength of the women who make them. The few antique pieces I have collected are small rectangular ceremonial cloths called gallas, worn to cover the nape of a Banjara woman's neck. I set them on a table as a centerpiece or hang them on the wall, treating them as the true works of art that they are.

I love telling stories by grouping objects together. Creating vignettes on bookshelves, nestling tiny mementos among books, breaks up the monotony of rows of books. Placing items of varying shapes and heights asymmetically keeps things relaxed and more interesting.

DESIGN NOTES
## Collecting

This is a book about nature, and when it comes to the whole nature versus nurture debate, it seems almost genetic predisposition that my son Hugo would have turned out to be a collector and plant lover just like me. He likes dark greens, browns, earthy prints, and ancient relics. He's an avid collector, filling his room with revered statues, artifacts, and tribal masks. There's always a smell of incense wafting out from the crack beneath his door as well as the sound of music—everything from jazz to rap to funk, and, to my amusement (and not-so-secret delight), disco. I'll hear him practicing trumpet, drums, or piano or recording beats in his closet-turned-recording studio. While his tastes are eclectic, they are all grounded in a deep, rich appreciation of history and nature. His room feels very much *him*: down-to-earth, rooted, filled with plants and books on history and other cultures. My fern-print wallpaper, which he chose, hangs on one of his walls, the charcoal gray background with the gold fern print perfectly matches the earthy vibe of his room.

The colors and tactility of the ornate embroidery and beading
on this wool coat remind me of fertile earth bursting with new
life. While I love wearing the coat, I get the most satisfaction
by hanging it on the coatrack in our entryway for all to view.

# WEEDS

Wild, unruly, tenacious; against all odds, weeds dwell in the margins, sprouting from any unlikely crevice. Chamomile nestled in the cracks of sidewalks, dandelion puffs poking their heads through the openings in chain-link fences, ethereal Queen Anne's lace spreading its shawl over an abandoned field. A few are celebrated and protected, like the golden orange California poppy, but most are considered commonplace, like the little yellow Bermuda buttercups dotting the roadsides.

They are the most overlooked form of natural beauty—unsung rebels in our midst, joyfully resisting the grayness of urban life.

Weeds are green grasses and brambly brown shoots. They are bushy bases with straggly stems and explosions of psychedelic wildflowers. These insistent things push boldly upward with life, reaching relentlessly toward the sun. They are the most overlooked form of natural beauty—unsung rebels in our midst, joyfully resisting the grayness of urban life.

When I'm driving on the freeway, I'm always amazed to see so many of them: fertile patches of fennel fronds and dandelions hugging the concrete shoulders of the road. The golden feathers of pampas grass dancing gracefully under the overpasses. Even the ones that look wispy and delicate are hearty enough to grow on a median between busy traffic lanes. These wild flora need no human help. No one has planted them—they have planted themselves.

Ivy vines scale the walls around my house. I watch as my neighbors rip the ivy down, peeling it back from the walls, because they don't like the way it takes over. But I love the way it takes over (within reason), how the tiny feet cling to the sides of homes and the way it voraciously climbs up and over fences. I like how it stakes its claim and overgrows, refusing to be confined.

And it isn't just the spirit of weeds that I admire, I love their unabashed beauty grown wild. The way they tangle up with one another. Their myriad surfaces, shapes, and hues inspire me to mix and match color, pattern, and texture in bold ways. The interplay of unexpected composition; the kaleidoscopic clashing colors—mixing plaids with paisley, stripes with florals. I have an affinity for patterns that run rampant like the ivy on my walls.

A weed is just an unwanted plant, which means any plant, really, can be considered a weed. I love the idea of something that's unwanted being a source of beauty. The way in which weeds are overlooked as worthy flora reminds me of the shaggy, colorful Boucherouite rag rugs I've been collecting over the years. Made from scraps of discarded fabric and clothing, these bright-colored, scrappy mats, with their stripes, diamond-shapes, and zigzag patterns, show how beautiful things can be created out of materials that would otherwise be tossed.

A weed is just an unwanted plant, which means any plant, really, can be considered a weed. I love the idea of something that's unwanted being a source of beauty.

I have a favorite weed that lives in the parking lot behind my store on Fourth Street in Berkeley. I noticed it one day, growing out of the bolt hole in one of the parking space's concrete wedges. From its dime-size planter pot, this perfect little thing grows forth, its green-and-pink-tinged shoots and Lilliputian yellow flowers nurtured by nothing more than a few drops of rain. It's my secret talisman; it's this ability to thrive unnoticed, bursting ahead with such life and determination from such a small space, that inspires me. This tiny weed reminds me to be strong and resilient. Since the early days of starting my business, I've always made the most from what's available to me—decorating my stores with flea-market and salvage-yard finds, using things like wrought-iron scrap metal as clothing racks and bamboo as curtain rods—things I still do today. Sometimes the constraints of having fewer resources forces one to be more innovative in the things you gather and surround yourself with.

I see weeds everywhere I go—waving hello from cracks in the sidewalk and throwing raucous parties for themselves in vacant lots. They are resilient, returning, always rising. Even though I find myself yanking weeds from areas in my garden, that doesn't stop me from admiring their strength and persistence. Even pulling out their roots, I know they'll somehow return. Their audacity has inspired me to boldly mix prints, patterns, colors, and textures, and their spirit frees my work from predictability. They have taught me to be stronger and wilder and to seek out beauty in unexpected places.

They have taught me to be stronger and wilder and to seek out beauty in unexpected places.

To me, emulating weeds means mixing patterns, prints, colors, and texture in unexpected ways. In my hallway, I combine two Osborne & Little wallpaper patterns with a bright zigzag Boucherouite rag rug. A glimpse of the bold 1960s Swedish graphic floral fabric-turned-shower curtain adds to the cacophony of pattern and color.

CUT EITHER ALONE
OR W/ CHIFFON
+ USE EXCESS FOR SCARVES

(WARPED
PISLEY)

When I began designing, I worked mostly with solid and striped fabrics, not favoring any of the prints offered by fabric mills. Once I found a resource to print my own designs onto fabric, my collections became much more free. I was able to pull inspiration from my surroundings and translate that into my work, creating original prints and mixing patterns, textures, and colors in exciting ways. My collections evolved from subtle, quiet palettes (which I still love) to include more elaborate and layered combinations.

The colorful, graphic 1960s curtains make the perfect backdrop
for this party setting. An assortment of jewel-toned glassware, a
bold slightly psychedelic print tablecloth, and foraged wildflowers
create a vibrant yet laid-back mood.

DESIGN NOTES
## The Beauty of Chaos

Just as every house has a junk drawer, there's often one room where the odds and ends and orphan objects reside. While I continually strive to declutter our house, there is one room where chaos and clutter reign supreme. Our "breakfast room" (though we have never eaten in there) is a small space where we keep our bags, craft supplies, cookbooks, wine, surplus dishes, and recycling bins. If we're not sure where to put it, it goes here. It's been home to bikes, scooters, skateboards, backpacks, and dog beds—a West Coast version of a mudroom. There are so many little things I keep, from magazines I can't seem to part with to shopping bags, ribbon, and colorful tape. I tidy this room now and then but mostly I just accept the chaos and clutter of it. I appreciate that all of these things that fill the room, while maybe less beautiful, have a place in our lives and I try to arrange this hodgepodge of items in a visually interesting way. I store things in open cubbies, sometimes coordinating them by color, to create some harmony amid the mayhem. I've accentuated the wild, colorful mess of the room by hanging and stacking bright oil paintings done by members of the family along with my overflow of colorful vintage lights to give a sense of joyful celebration. In the same way that I find unwanted weeds beautiful, I find the everyday objects that make life possible, from shopping totes to party streamers, worth celebrating and displaying with pride.

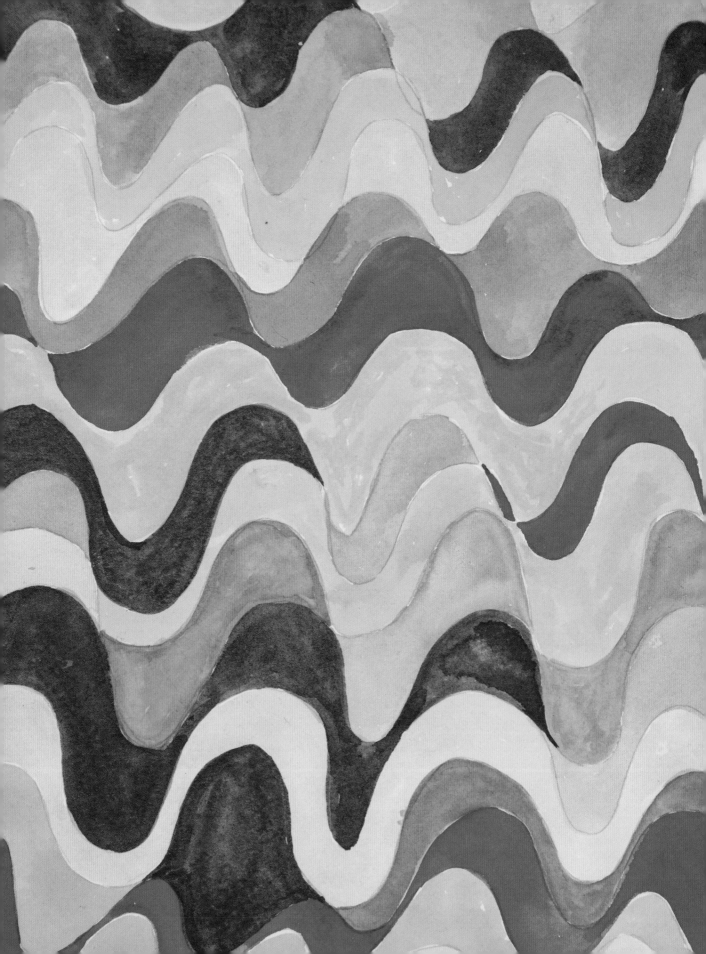

DESIGN NOTES
## Kids' Rooms

Kids' rooms are free spaces, or at least they should be. They have a sense of wild abandon to them and can be crazy and untamed. It's the place where children develop their sense of selves and their aesthetic sensibilities. As a kid, my room was the center of my creative world. The same goes for my daughter Isabelle's room, which started out an all-pink magical wonderland full of fairies and miniature worlds. As she's gotten older, she's managed to keep that loose and playful attitude toward decorating her room, while refining her aesthetic a bit yet retaining a magical, feminine feeling (fairies and deer still remain a love of hers). And even though the walls are still painted the pale pink from when she was little, her room has become more about playing with color and mixing patterns and prints. Quilts and pillows of many ethnicities and proudly displayed souvenirs from family trips and concerts exist alongside her artwork and artwork made by her friends. She blends cultures, eras, and themes—never worrying about them clashing. As long as she loves something, it will somehow work with everything else. It's her tendency to not overthink that creates such spontaneity in the room. We share an eclectic sensibility and belief that what you love defines your aesthetic, and over time the things you collect come to reflect your individual sense of taste.

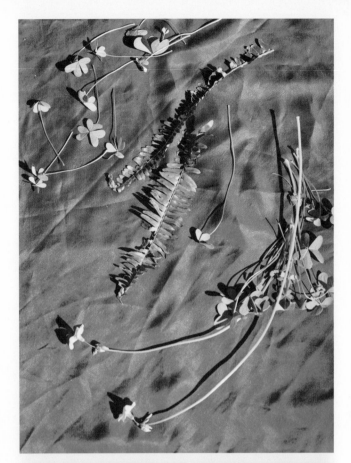

Ann Holsberry is a mixed-media painter whose work references the ephemeral aspects of the natural world. Cyanotype is a photographic process where photo-sensitive chemicals are applied to a surface and then objects are placed on that surface and exposed to light. The result is that the portion of the surface that is covered remains white, while the paper or fabric turns a deep Prussian blue. Ann's use of relics from the natural world—vines, feathers, ferns—and the way she places them on fabric with such a sense of poetry deeply resonated with me. The mercurial and unpredictable nature of the cyanotype process also intrigued me. It's completely dependent on the elements, weather, and light conditions. While the blue-and-white images are beautifully ethereal and dreamy, I was curious to see what would happen if we started with a different color base. I suggested this to Ann, who was excited by the prospect of experimenting with different colored silks and printing directly onto garments.

It felt like magic. The areas where Ann placed wild vines remained the fabric's original color while the rest turned a beautiful vibrant hue changed by the deep blue from the chemical reaction: fabric that started as aqua blue became a deeper blue, citron green turned into a vibrant forest green, and the fuchsia silk changed to a royal purple. The degree of darkening and saturation varied, depending on the weather and length of time the fabric was left exposed to sunlight. The process of creating cyanotypes is unpredictable, asking us to accept the factor of chance and respect the will of nature.

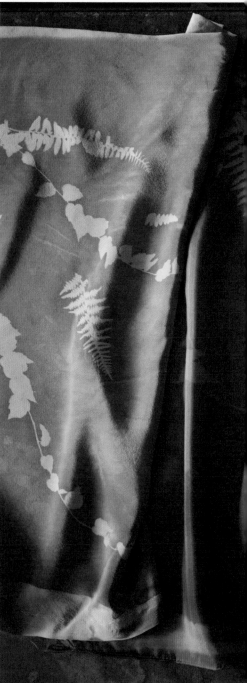

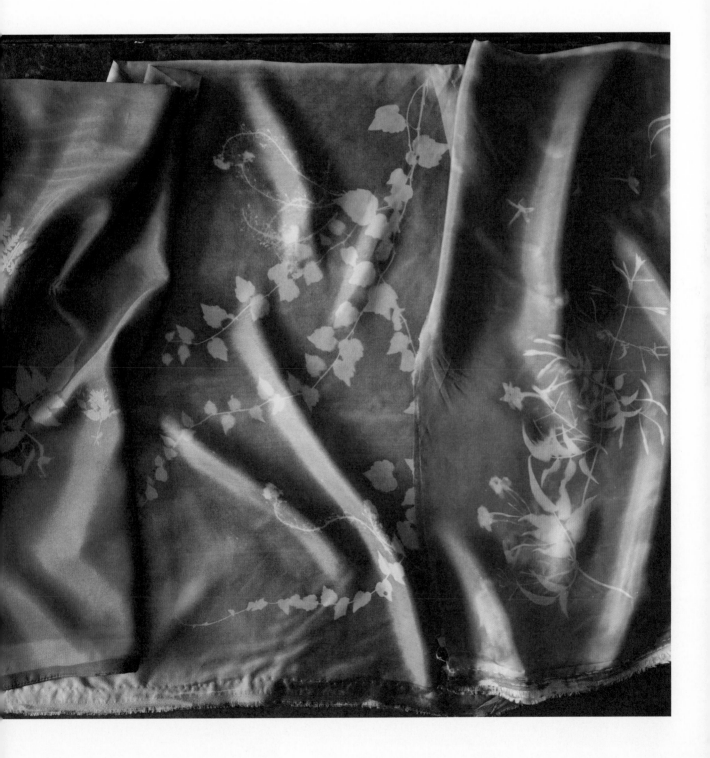

DESIGN NOTES
## Controlled Exuberance

Alayne Patrick is one of my oldest, dearest friends. We met in San Francisco years ago, at a clothing store where we both worked. We hit it off right away, soon discovered we shared a passion for flea marketing, and started collecting for a store we thought we might open together one day. I moved to New York for school, Alayne joined a few years later, and for a while we shared an apartment where we deepened our love of hunting for beautiful old things and then arranging them.

Over the years, we've each developed our own style, but a certain shared aesthetic remains and is a definite bond between us. Alayne's style tends to be more minimal and tidy while mine is more loose and bohemian. We both have a deep appreciation (and possible hoarding tendency) for antique textiles; Alayne's collection is composed mostly from her travels to India and Central Asia. Stacks of neatly folded colorful linens line her closets—a rainbow of Indian saris laced with gold, heavily embroidered floral Suzani tribal cloths, and, my favorite, hand-loomed cotton from Pakistan's Swat region, intricately embroidered with bright silk thread, most often in shades of pink—which happens to be a color we both love. Hot pink to be exact.

Alayne recently bought a charming 1925 wood-shingled house on Long Island, an ideal refuge from the city, which she is thoughtfully and carefully restoring. Everything is in the details—from a tiny, intricately carved silver-and-ebony acorn that hangs on a doorknob to the installation of period-appropriate fixtures throughout the rooms. The entire house reflects her refined minimalist style and attention to specifics. I especially love the shock of the neon pink stripe in her bathroom, dividing the white top half of the walls and pale blush of the bottom half. Such a simple yet impactful feature in an otherwise serene room; the use of the color is so striking and surprisingly perfect.

embroidery from india & pakistan   Sheila Paine

EDITIONS BACHARI

LA CALLIGRAPHIE ARABE

One, Two, Tree!   Ravishankar/Rao/Durga Bai

Traditional Textiles of Central Asia   JANET HARVEY

Decorate   Holly Becker & Joanna Copestick

TRADITIONAL KALAMKARI   LES INDIENNES

THE MOSQUE   EDITED BY MARTIN FRISHMAN AND HASAN-UDDIN KHAN

TEXTILES OF THE WIENER WERKSTÄTTE 1910-1932

NewDelhiNewWave

Costume, Textiles and Jewellery of INDIA
Traditions in Rajasthan   Vandana Bhandari

Sometimes just letting things be, rather than
deliberately arranging, is best. Channeling
the way weeds haphazardly grow, nothing is
contrived.

Feathery plumes of pampas grass that grow wild along the freeway
inspire the mood of this bedroom. The shaggy Turkish Tulu textile
at the foot of the bed combined with an early-American crazy quilt–
turned–pillow cover, an embroidered Pakistani pillow from the Swat
region, and shams made from Peruvian mantas create a free-spirited
yet decadent vibe.

# DECAY

A bouquet of flowers slowly wilts on my nightstand; the once lush and brightly colored blooms begin to wither. Stark whites become elegant creams. Bright pinks fade into dusty mauve. The petals become thin and papery, falling delicately from the stem. I always have flowers around my home, whether cut from my garden or purchased from a flower shop. Instead of discarding them at the first sign of wilting, I usually wait until they are fully dried before tossing them. I like to watch them gently turn, their brilliant colors dimming, the petals gracefully crumpling and bending, taking on new shapes

*It's the process of decay that intrigues me. There is a sense of relaxed beauty that can come only with age.*

and silhouettes. Rose petals dry out and fall, leaving little upturned floral cups. Hydrangeas become starched, more complex versions of their younger selves. A peony opens completely in full bloom and then each petal demurely curls up on itself before dropping. While I adore a blossom still in its tight bud or at the peak of its short life, its wilting stages are equally compelling. I am drawn to the gentle process of slowly fading away.

Outside, beautiful decay is everywhere. Tea-stained scabiosa pods take on Victorian poise out in the fields—equally captivating dried as in bloom. Dead sunflowers, once bright yellow, now shine like bronzed circles of dehydrated honeycomb. A painted wall weathered by the elements turns into a peeling, layered work of art. Each becomes something different, and is still beautiful to me.

*We are taught to worship the new but I find myself repeatedly pulled to things that show signs of age and time. Things in a state of disrepair. There is so much beauty to be found in objects that have naturally changed course.*

It's the process of decay that intrigues me. There is a sense of relaxed beauty that can come only with age. A fallen ivy leaf left to the elements will gradually decompose, leaving only a thin skeletal framework, veins as delicate as lace, reminding me of the intricate crocheted curtains in my bedroom. An old silver pitcher can become so tarnished it looks as if it's been draped with a night rainbow, in deep blacks, iridescent purples, and shiny blues. We are taught to worship the new but I find myself repeatedly pulled to things that show signs of age and time. Things in a state of disrepair. There is so much beauty to be found in objects that have naturally changed course.

I love the way fabrics fade in color; bold lines become whispered hieroglyphics and floral prints fade away almost completely to ghost-like sketches. Edges begin to fray, making delicate fringe. I often re-create this fraying effect of worn textiles by leaving the edges raw on pieces in my clothing collection or intentionally making fringe by pulling out some of the fibers. I also use the ragged selvage of a fabric as a finishing detail. I have even designed prints with a faded color palette to echo these time-worn effects.

I believe that including objects with history in your home lends it some soul.

I tend to create interior spaces that have a familiar sense of lived-in ease. Rooms that are thoughtfully undone, lined with faded leather chairs, worn prayer rugs, peeling painted portraits, reveal lives well lived. My own home's history and personality is embodied in time-worn things—hand-painted wallpaper, fraying kilim rugs, artwork by family and friends both living and not. You can feel the people who have lived here, the paths their feet have traveled along the distressed floorboards, replete with scratches and dings. I believe that including objects with history in your home lends it some soul. Things with rich patina express the beauty and depth of having lived through many seasons; they convey a sense of ease and wisdom, a gentle comfort with their surroundings.

I also believe in giving things new life. So often, people want to toss objects at the first sign of wear or decay, but this is when I feel inspired to reuse them, or give them a new context or form. Visibly patching a worn textile full of holes can extend its life with new charm, as will using the parts that remain intact to make something altogether different, such as a patchwork spread or a decorative pillow. I've used the pages of a vintage book to wallpaper a room. Appreciating the degradation and transformation of something, seeing that beauty, is paramount.

I cherish these things that are on the verge of being gone; they are so elegant in these stages of transformation, wistful and tender as they fade away.

I cherish these things that are on the verge of being gone; they are so elegant in these stages of transformation, wistful and tender as they fade away.

I still find the horsehair upholstery, split and ravaged by age, of this gothic settee to be beautiful. I can't bear to reupholster it. I feel the same way about the worn steps in my studio. I love seeing the progression of color as each layer wears away, revealing the history of the building. Just as I adore the delicate, ghost-like texture and patterns that the clinging roots of ivy leave behind.

## Fleeting Beauty

I have an affinity for magnolias, especially at the onset of spring when the blossoms form on the bare branches. It always makes me catch my breath to see the extraordinary explosion of stark white, pale blush, and deep pink flowers throughout the neighborhood. We have a *Magnolia stellata*—sometimes called star magnolia—in our backyard, a gift that came with the house, planted by the previous owner. Its flowers are a magnificent pure cream tinged with the palest blush, releasing the most delicate fragrance. I find the way each flower unfurls from its cottony bud, the white petals curling downward in almost crinkled-like fashion, having the effect of a wilting bloom from the onset, so endearing. Even the youngest flower has a tender fragile appearance, already hinting at the end of its lifespan. Magnolias have been the subject of much adulation and exploration in my work; one of my pencil drawings of the stellata tree, touched with watercolors, became a print for clothing and bedding. Perhaps one day I'll create a wallpaper from this stellata print, so I can be surrounded by the flower's beauty year-round.

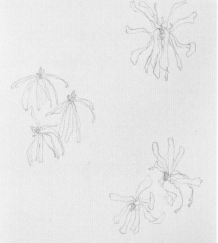

The delicate veins of a decomposing ivy leaf so closely resemble
lace that it's hard to imagine the genesis of the latter could have
come from any other form or inspiration. The intricate antique
curtain, found at an estate sale and now hanging in my bedroom,
perfectly echoes the skeletal form of the leaf.

A dead pine tree stands tall in my neighborhood. Its stoic, graceful limbs create an eerily stark and somber silhouette against the fog, reminding me of intricate lace.

The quiet melancholy of this still life is punctuated with a simple glass bottle holding daffodils past their prime.

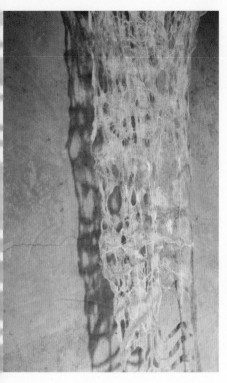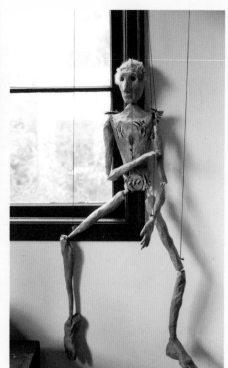

## The Art of Reuse

My daughter, Isabelle, is blessed with a unique combination of pragmatism and creativity. She loves working with her hands, making things. She hates waste and prefers using found objects or materials that would otherwise be thrown away or recycled, and is a master at creating beauty from objects that seemingly have no value.

One of her installations at school was a huge grid of used tea bags. She saved her tea bags over a long period of time, letting them dry out, and then used them to create a beautiful wall of varying shades of sepia. The effect was serene, stunningly graphic, and provided a new context for something used and considered done.

Her sculptures made of wire, cardboard, paper, tape, feathers—anything she finds interesting and useful—are unexpectedly alive. I'm moved by how much humanness she creates in a face that isn't human. I love that such simple and easily acquired materials create such beauty, whimsy, and richness. Her ability to give discarded objects—those past their prime—new life and meaning continues to inspire me.

DESIGN NOTES
## Storied Walls

I have a beautiful vintage book titled, *Know Thyself: Nature's Secrets Revealed*, dated 1912, that I probably picked up at a flea market when I lived in New York. It's a guidebook of sorts, providing "Help and Instruction for Every Member of Every Home"; with chapters ranging from "Etiquette" and "How to Be Beautiful" to "Love, Adaptation and Courtship," "Marriage," and "Child-Bearing." As you can imagine, most of the "counsel" is extremely outdated. Some of the advice is appalling, but most is simply amusing ("A dirty neck and smiling face are not in harmony" and "Every lady owes it to herself to be fascinating"). The edition had

been a continuous source of entertainment for the whole family but was falling apart; the cover had separated from the spine and I kept it tied together with a ribbon. Recently I thought, "What better way to preserve and enjoy this book than to use the pages to wallpaper the powder room?" I carefully separated the pages from the binding and arranged them to cover the walls. Now everyone can read their favorite passages while in the bathroom, without having to hold the crumbling tome in their hands. The walls provide great dinner conversation when friends are over and make a visit to the WC.

Muted colors, fraying edges, missing beads, fading
flowers, peeling paint—I am drawn to things that
epitomize beautiful decay.

DESIGN NOTES
## Tarnishing Beauty

When I opened my San Francisco store, many years ago, I wanted to wallpaper the back wall of the jewel-box space, which had high boxed-beamed ceilings and intricate medallion wood work. The space needed something magnificent to anchor its small yet regal aesthetic. After scouring every wallpaper showroom and almost giving up, I discovered the most beautiful hand-painted botanical chinoiserie scene on silver-leafed silk by De Gournay, featuring a garden of dogwood, tree peonies, exotic birds, and butterflies. The bright, shimmering metallic of the silver-leaf background gave it the subtle opulence and grandeur that I love. It was truly exquisite and, of course, extremely expensive. The cost was astronomical for me. I was used to designing spaces on a limited budget. But this wallpaper was different. It was *perfect*. So beautiful it made my heart ache. I took the plunge.

Because it had to be custom hand-painted, I knew the timing was going to be tight for the opening of my store. As I feared, the wallpaper arrived about a month too late. Although I was hugely disappointed at first, I believe fate took its course. The thought of putting up something so expensive and permanent on the wall of a space that I might one day leave started to weigh on me. Knowing that the next occupant might tear it down or paint over it crushed me. So, once the wallpaper arrived, I decided to hold on to it rather than install it in the shop—for what, I wasn't sure.

It wasn't until my family moved into our 1926 Mediterranean fixer-upper in the Berkeley Hills that the wallpaper found its home. By some miracle, it was the exact width of my new bedroom wall. The effect was breathtaking. I felt like a fairy living among kingfishers and butterflies in a garden of flowering trees.

The showroom had warned me that the silver background, while shiny and bright to begin with, would naturally tarnish and darken with age, especially when exposed to sunlight. That made it all the more enticing to me. Our bedroom is so sunny that the tarnishing began pretty quickly; the silver first turned a rose color and then darkened just as a sterling pitcher will if not polished. A beautiful and inconsistent iridescent rainbow of pinks, purples, greens, and blues emerged, all with a pewter hue lurking behind.

It's been up ten years now, and I'm sure it will be up at least another ten. The wallpaper is constantly evolving, bringing with it a new life for each of its stages. Allowing and appreciating the change and patina that comes with age is what I love. The darkening progression seems magical. I love watching the garden wall gracefully change with time.

One of my favorite vintage-shop finds is an old hand-painted
silk lantern that hangs in my home studio. The fading roses,
as well as the disintegrating fabric on which they're painted,
are like wilted roses just before the petals fall.

This 1970s wall hanging, space-dyed
and ruggedly woven, gives the ravaged
appearance of something that has
been around forever, which I love. It
reminds me of tattered ship sails or
the beauty of decomposing leaves.

DESIGN NOTES
## Layered History

When we moved into our 1926 Mediterranean home ten years ago, there was a lot of work that needed to be done. One job was ripping out the built-in cabinets, which had been installed in the 1980s, in what would be our sitting room. Once they came down, we discovered layers of paint and plaster from previous lives along with the penciled notations left behind by the craftsmen who constructed and installed the cabinets. While my original plan was to paint or possibly wallpaper the space, once I saw the history of the room, the measurements and scrawled carpenter notes marking the decisions of the former owners, I knew I wanted to leave them exposed rather than paint them over. It was too endearing and beautiful to cover up. Without intending to, we had unveiled stories—the coded communications between contractors—that were now part of *our* story.

Look closely.

The beautiful may be small.

—IMMANUEL KANT

### DESIGN NOTES
## Fading Grandeur

Quite a few years ago, an antique-textile dealer, from whom I had bought several pieces in the past, contacted me, letting me know she had a pair of nineteenth-century Chinese panels she thought I'd be interested in. I was not expecting anything quite so stunning. She unrolled the long, exquisite purply blue duchesse silk panels laden with embroidered wisteria and butterflies in flight. They took my breath away. While I had no immediate use for them, I knew they were too special to pass up. I bought them and put them in a trunk, and waited for the perfect moment to unveil them. That moment came in 2010 when I opened a store in Marin.

The store's warm, natural color scheme and high ceilings made it the perfect space to showcase the panels, which would be used as dressing-room curtains. They were magnificent! With continued use and exposure to light, however, the silk has begun to deteriorate. The embroidered areas stayed intact, while the fabric base began to shred. We reinforced the back of the curtains where we could but otherwise let the natural progression of decay happen. Still beautiful, the texture and color changed alongside the continued disintegration of the fibers, becoming something altogether different—ravaged beauty.

Although it does sadden me to watch the degeneration of the curtains— seeing them become mere threads, ghosts of their former selves—I don't regret hanging them. I love that so many people got to experience the beauty of these works of art. I believe it's important to use our treasures and let others enjoy them as well, even if it means their lives are cut short by wear and tear. Surrounding ourselves with beauty, savoring each moment and appreciating every phase of life is key. It's poignant to witness the natural decomposing until no life remains. Nature has taught me this.

# LIFE CYCLE OF A PRINT

Most of this book is about how nature inspires me, sometimes literally but often loosely, and the abstract correlations between nature and my designs. There is, however, a necessary translation of inspiration to object, and here I'll walk you step-by-step through the stages of one of my prints—from first sight to sketching to choosing colors and fabrics to the final products—so you can see how nature directly informs my design process.

## Inspiration

I'm obsessed with ferns. There is something otherworldly about the way they unfurl and extend their furry brown fronds and delicate green tendrils. I'm always amazed at the way they're able to grow out of tree trunks and stone walls, and am enchanted by the lacy patterns they make on the ground when light shines through them. I've planted dozens of different types of ferns throughout my yard, each one offering its own miraculous shape, color, and growth pattern.

I've always seen the ground as a stage for the shadow play of plants and trees. I love the way ferns cast themselves on surfaces, their dark silhouettes swaying lazily against the rich brown earth. I have a group of potted plants on my front porch, mostly succulents and ferns mixed with a boronia and *Michelia platypetala*, both incredibly fragrant when in bloom—I love how the shapes and textures blend with one another. There is one particular fern, an Australian tree fern, that creates a beautiful shadow against the concrete surface of the porch. Each morning, I admire the fern's shadow. It lasts for only a couple of hours and then disappears. One day, I decided to finally sit down and draw it.

## Exploration

I went outside with a large piece of paper, setting it down directly on the stoop so the shadow would fall upon it. The shadow created such a bold silhouette—one I thought would translate beautifully onto fabric. Once I had traced the intricate outline of the fern, I colored it in with pencil, to mimic the actual shadow's form.

## Orientation

I wanted this print to be rich and sultry but also a bit bold and graphic, all while maintaining the delicacy of the outline of the fern. I knew keeping the actual size of the fern (about 11 inches long) would give the impact I was after. In choosing colors, I didn't necessarily want to be literal, like green on a brown background or even black and gray as, at first glance, the fern shadow appeared on my porch. Instead, I wanted to capture the richness and depth of the shadow the fern made; not the fern itself. I chose earthy, subtle colors—ecru, dark chocolate, and amber to offset the bold size and pattern.

## Material Selection

Playing with texture, color, patterns, and prints is my idea of heaven. It's my favorite part of the design process. I need to sit and live with the fabrics for a while before deciding what I want to make with them—determining which styles and silhouettes are best suited for the fabrics I've selected. I chose to print the fern on silk crepe de chine, which has a slightly sueded hand and a nice weight and drape to it. I knew the colors on silk would be richly saturated. The fern print was part of my winter 2014 collection. The other fabrics in the collection were quite textural and opulent—French fringed tapestry, a metallic gold raffia-like fabric, and a delicately sequined-striped raw silk—so I didn't need more fabrics that would add shimmer, I had enough of that happening. I preferred the idea of balancing the decadent fabrics of the collection with something a bit more subtle, yet still luxurious. The matte and saturated nature of silk crepe de chine would provide that.

## Fruition

### CLOTHING

Once deciding to print on silk crepe de chine, I chose clothing styles from my archives that would work well in silk—simple yet fluid silhouettes to show off the fabric's natural character. I was careful to select styles without a lot of seams, to avoid breaking up the large fern pattern. I wanted the motif to stay intact as much as possible on each garment.

### HOME FURNISHINGS

I wanted ferns everywhere, so I also had the pattern printed on a heavy Belgian linen to use for drapes, upholstery, cushions, and table linens. I limited the silk screening to one color option and chose a metallic gold ink to be printed on a natural linen background—earthy with a touch of glamour.

### WALLPAPER

I love wallpaper. I've used it quite a bit in my own home, even if just on a single wall in a room. When I decided to dive in to the world of designing wallpaper, the fern print was my immediate first choice. I thought it would translate beautifully and dramatically onto walls. I scaled up the print a bit so the image could have more impact. I wanted to continue with the rich, sultry color palette I had chosen for the silk fabric while adding a bit of extravagance with metallics. I chose five combinations: chocolate/platinum, charcoal/gold, cream/gold, charcoal/chocolate, and cream/chocolate. Earthy, bold, and subtly glamorous, these five colorways brought out the depth and opulence I was after when first drawing the shadow of the fern on my front porch.

# RESOURCES

## SHOPPING

### A DETACHER

Mona Kowalska's jewel-box store featuring her cerebral clothing collection and a curated selection of home goods.

adetacher.com
185 Mulberry Street
New York, NY 10012

### ATOMIC GARDEN

An eclectic and bountiful selection of home goods.

atomicgardenoakland.com
5453 College Avenue
Oakland, CA 94618

### BERKELEY HORTICULTURAL NURSERY

A well organized nursery with a large selection of plants and a friendly and knowledgeable staff.

berkeleyhort.com
1310 McGee Avenue
Berkeley, CA 94703

### CHAIRISH

An online marketplace of vintage and used home furnishings.

chairish.com

### CHRIS HOWARD ANTIQUES & MODERN

Stunning mid-century furniture.

antiquesandmodern.com
3017 Adeline Street
Berkeley, CA 94703

### CLARS AUCTION GALLERY

Antique auction house.

clars.com

### EBAY

An online auction for almost anything.

eBay.com

### ERICA TANOV

A carefully curated selection of clothing and home goods featuring Erica Tanov collections alongside select designers and artisans.

ericatanov.com
1827 4th Street
Berkeley, CA 94710

•

2415 Larkspur Landing Circle
Larkspur, CA 94939

•

1318 E 7th Street #120
Los Angeles, CA 90021

### ETSY

An online marketplace specializing in handmade and vintage items.

etsy.com

### FAR & FEW

Vintage clothing and objets d'art.

1643 San Pablo Avenue
Berkeley, CA 94702

### 1st DIBS

1stdibs.com

### FLOWERLAND

My favorite nursery and gift shop and also home to the highwire coffee Airstream trailer.

flowerlandshop.com
1330 Solano Avenue
Albany, CA 94706

### JOHN DERIAN

Decoupage, unusual ephemera, and home accessories both antique and new.

johnderian.com
6 E 2nd Street
New York, NY 10003

### LAYLA

Astounding collection of textiles, towels, and jewelry predominantly from India.

layla-bklyn.com
352 Atlantic Avenue
Brooklyn, NY 11217

### MAROC TRIBAL

Extensive selection of Moroccan rugs.

maroctribal.com

### MICHELE VARIAN

Modern, minimal, and eclectic home decor.

michelevarian.com
27 Howard Street
New York, NY 10013

### MONOGRAPH BOOKWERKS

Rare vintage books and relics.

monographbookwerks.com
500 NE 27th Avenue
Portland, OR 97211

## OHMEGA SALVAGE

Well-organized salvage yard and a good source for vintage hardware and bric-a-brac.

ohmegasalvage.com
2400 San Pablo Avenue
Berkeley, CA 94702

## PARCEL

Magical shop of fine paper goods and vintage ephemera.

shopparcel.com
608 Bloomfield Avenue
Montclair, NJ 07042

## PILSEN COMMUNITY BOOKS

Beautifully curated new and used bookstore.

pilsencommunitybooks.org
1102 W 18th Street
Chicago, IL 60608

## TAIL OF THE YAK

A whimsical shop full of treasures and curiosities.

2632 Ashby Avenue
Berkeley, CA 94705

## TINSEL TRADING

Antique trims and ephemera.

tinseltrading.com
1659 San Pablo Avenue
Berkeley, CA 94702

## URBAN ORE

Salvaged doors, furniture, and assorted items.

urbanore.com
900 Murray Street
Berkeley, CA 94710

# FLEA MARKETS

## ALAMEDA FLEA MARKET

alamedapointantiquesfaire.com

## ALEMANY FLEA MARKET

100 Alemany Boulevard
San Francisco, CA 94110

## BRIMFIELD ANTIQUE AND COLLECTIBLES SHOW

Largest outdoor antiques fair in the United States—three times a year.

brimfieldshow.com
Route 20
Brimfield, MA 01010

## BROOKLYN FLEA

brooklynflea.com

## PORTE DE CLIGNANCOURT FLEA MARKET

"LE MARCHÉ AUX PUCES DE SAINT-OUEN"

marcheauxpuces-saintouen.com/1.aspx
Paris, France

# ARCHITECTURE + DESIGN

## ALL ROADS DESIGN

allroadsdesign.com

## CLE TILE

cletile.com

## DE GOURNAY

degournay.com

## ENVELOPE A+D

envelopead.com

## GUSTAVE CARSLON DESIGN

gustavecarlsondesign.com

## HERRON

studioherron.com

## MCEWEN LIGHTING STUDIO

mcewenlighting.com

## OSBORNE & LITTLE

osborneandlittle.com

# ARTISTS

## AKIO NUKAGA

akio-nukaga.com

## ALEXANDER KORI GIRARD

alexanderkorigirard.com

## ANN HOLSBERRY

annholsberry.com

## CAROLINE SECKINGER

carolineseckinger.com

## CREATIVE GROWTH

creativegrowth.org

## EMILY PAYNE

emilypayneart.com

## KELLY ORDING

kellyording.com

## LENA WOLFF

lenawolff.com

## NATIVE LINE

nativeline.com

## ACKNOWLEDGMENTS

Making this book was a momentous endeavor for me, full of many firsts. There are so many people who supported me throughout the process for whom I'm forever grateful and owe my sincerest thanks.

To my husband, Steven Emerson, for pushing me to give my all, and lifting me up when I was doubting myself. And for putting up with my taking over the house for the past year and a half (and maybe always). Your patience, love, and understanding mean the world to me.

To my dad, who ignited my love and appreciation for nature with our weekend hikes and instilling in me a keen sense of observation. My mom, who has always believed in me . . . sometimes embarrassingly too much. And my stepfather, John, for his constant support and questioning.

To my sister, Eden. My big sis who has always taken care of me and remembers everything. Thank you for reminding me of some of the sweetest memories.

Ngoc Minh Ngo, who gave so much of herself to this project. Your gentle manner and sensitive eye were paramount to the book. I truly admire and appreciate your tireless energy and the soulful photographs you take. I cherish the time we spent together on our shoots and the deep friendship that blossomed.

Endless gratitude to the intuitive and gifted Anisse Gross, who helped put my thoughts, ideas, and musings into words. Your humor and deep understanding somehow made the writing process bearable.

To the Ten Speed team for believing in this book, and especially my editor, Jenny Wapner, who understood my vision and calmly held my hand through the process, offering great insight to make the book even better. And Emma Campion, who worked so closely with me on the design of the book, hearing my ideas and wishes and then taking them beyond my hopes and dreams. And to Jane Chinn, for making sure the materials were perfect.

To my agent, Kitty Cowles, who enthusiastically spearheaded the book and guided me through the process with her expertise.

To Leilani Labong, my coconspirator in conceptualizing the book and crafting the proposal over many iced teas together.

To Remi Abbas for listening, brainstorming, and offering your words of wisdom.

To Coralie Langston-Jones, my publicist, friend, and muse who makes my clothing look so good. Your poise and grace are an inspiration.

To Gabrielle Stiles and Lauren Ardis, my studio dream team, who held down the fort while I was away on shoots and entrenched in writing. You two are my beautiful anchors whose talent and dedication are deeply appreciated.

I am eternally grateful for my brilliant store managers, Eline Johannessen and Caroline Jurovic, who kept the stores sailing smoothly while I was deeply immersed in the project and couldn't give my full attention. And to the rest of the ET family for your enthusiasm and devotion. Each one of you brings so much to the company. I could not do any of this without you.

To Alayne Patrick, Anne Marxer and Chris Heine, Caroline Seckinger and Gustave Carlson, Coralie and Brett Wickens, Erin Hiemstra, Katy Grannan and John McNeil, Max Gill, and Melissa Gomes and Michael McEwen, who generously opened their beautiful homes to me.

Boundless love and appreciation to artists Emily Payne, Caroline Seckinger, Kelly Ording, Lena Wolff, Ann Holsberry, Janelle Pietrzak, and Sierra Reading, who shared their studios and creativity with me and opened me up to the rich world of collaboration. I've learned so much and am deeply inspired by you all.

Thank you to my dear friends Liz, Birdie, Emily, Caroline, Missy, Nan, Hannah, Alayne, Rae, Jessie, Erin, Katy, Nel, and Amy, who offered so much encouragement and always lent an ear or eye.

And, of course, Hugo and Isabelle, my greatest pride and joy and always a source of true inspiration. You two put everything into perspective. I feel extraordinarily blessed to be your mother.

## ABOUT THE AUTHOR

Erica Tanov launched her eponymous label in 1990 after earning a BFA in fashion design from Parsons School of Design. Her collections of clothing and lifestyle goods, sold at her three boutiques in California and her online shop, epitomize relaxed luxury. Her work has been featured in *Vogue, Elle Decoration UK, Undecorate,* and *The New Bohemians.* Actresses including Maggie Gyllenhaal, Tilda Swinton, and Vera Farmiga have donned Tanov's enduring pieces.

Published in the United States by Ten Speed Press, an imprint of the Crown Publishing Group, a division of Penguin Random House LLC, New York.
www.crownpublishing.com
www.tenspeed.com

Ten Speed Press and the Ten Speed Press colophon are registered trademarks of Penguin Random House LLC.

Library of Congress Cataloging-in-Publication Data is on file with the publisher.

Hardcover ISBN: 978-0-399-57907-3
eBook ISBN: 978-0-399-57908-0

Printed in China

Design by Emma Campion

10 9 8 7 6 5 4 3 2 1

First Edition